This Too Shall Pass

A Young Woman's Recovery from Eating Disorders, Addictions, and Codependency

DAGMAR EVA KUSIAK

This Too Shall Pass
A Young Woman's Recovery from Eating Disorders, Addictions, and Codependency

Copyright © 2019 by Dagmar Eva Kusiak

Published by Clay Bridges in Houston, TX
www.ClayBridgesPublishing.com

All rights reserved. No part of this publication may be reproduced, stored in a retrieval system, or transmitted in any form by any means, electronic, mechanical, photocopy, recording, or otherwise, without the prior permission of the publisher, except as provided for by USA copyright law.

ISBN-10: 1-939815-68-1
ISBN-13: 978-1-939815-68-2
eISBN-10: 1-939815-64-9
eISBN-13: 978-1-939815-64-4

Special Sales: Most Clay Bridges titles are available in special quantity discounts. Custom imprinting or excerpting can also be done to fit special needs. Contact Clay Bridges at Info@ClayBridgesPublishing.com.

"Dagmar Kusiak has a story to tell. She has gone through a lot, survived it, and gone a whole lot further. Her poetry shows both her pain and her recovery in ways that can help us all. Her level of vulnerability is astonishing. Her honesty is remarkable. And her work shows how redemptive art can be."

—**Ginger Moran**, PhD
Author of *The Algebra of Snow*, Professor of Creative Writing at the University of Virginia

"Dagmar Kusiak does perhaps the bravest thing anyone could do. She peels back the layers of pain and hope to discover who and what are underneath it all. Inviting the reader to feel the weight of carrying 'ten thousand pounds of pain,' she punches holes in the darkness to discover a light that guides, comforts, and heals. This collection of poetry invites the reader to look at our own beginnings and endings—finding a strength beyond our own knowing."

—**Rev. Melissa Maher**

"Dagmar Kusiak has created a collection of poems that acts as a wise guide through the valley of pain, heartbreak, addiction, and struggle. These poems are raw and immediate, shining a light into dark places and ultimately giving hope in the struggle. In her vulnerability and honesty, Kusiak bears witness to the truth that through recovery, we can become strong in broken places."

—**Rev. Matthew H. Russell**, PhD

To All Women

*Who kept telling me, "Keep Coming Back,"
Cherished me before I could love myself,
Encouraged me when I felt weak,
And shared with me their most vulnerable self.
I love you all.*

Table of Contents

Introduction	1
Feelings: February 12, 2015	5
Journey: February 21, 2015	7
Create Your Story: February 25, 2015	9
On My Own: April 11, 2015	11
Go Away: April 12, 2015	13
Mother's Day: May 10, 2015	15
Labyrinth: May 11, 2015	17
Genie in a Bottle: May 22, 2015	19
Goodbyes: June 24, 2015	21
Grandma's Birthday: July 4, 2015	23
Who Am I: July 27, 2015	25
Tired of Losing: August 23, 2015	28
Love from a Parent's Point of View: September 2, 2015	30
The Sponsor: September 21, 2015	32
Let Go: October 4, 2015	34
Goodbye, Scale: October 5, 2015	36
Off the Wagon: October 29, 2015	38
Maggie: November 13, 2015	40
Cry for Help: November 19, 2015	42
Relapse: December 6, 2015	44
Sensei: December 6, 2015	46

Friendship: December 18, 2015	48
Carma: January 3, 2016	50
You Don't Know Me, Boss: January 7, 2016	52
Missing You: March 30, 2016	55
Dayenu: June 19, 2016	57
A Thousand Pounds: November 25, 2016	58
Note to Daggie – Reunion with Mom: November 28, 2016	60
Lost Child: December 15, 2016	61
New Chapter, New Sponsor: March 21, 2017	62
Before I Turn 40: August 24, 2017	63
I Am Available: August 27, 2017	64
Hurricane Harvey: August 27, 2017	66
My Meds: October 16, 2017	68
Freedom: October 17, 2017	69
Eyes Wide Shut: October 18, 2017	71
I Commit to You (God): October 19, 2017	73
Dating Again – When I Date Again: October 23, 2017	75
Loving Letter to Me: October 23, 2017	76
Georgia from Childhood: October 24, 2017	77
A Wall, No Intimacy: November 8, 2018	79
Sitting in Fear: November 11, 2018	81
Where Are You, God? November 12, 2018	83
Trust the Recovery Process: November 15, 2018	84
Growing Up: November 18, 2018	85
Connecting with Others: November 30, 2018	86
Future Story: December 21, 2018	87
Resources for Addiction Issues	89
A Note about the Author	91

Introduction

To love herself, every woman must learn to be herself.

1. "Feelings" is when I allowed myself to feel the enormous pain after my ex-fiancé and I broke off our engagement. This was the start of my spiritual journey.

2. "Journey" is a dialogue between self and new self. New self teaches and encourages how to sit with suffering and move away from it slowly.

3. "Create Your Story," "On My Own," and "Go Away" discuss the challenge of sitting still with uncomfortable feelings, becoming aware, and accepting these feelings without judgment.

4. "Mother's Day" is about the grief of not talking to my mom after I chose to take a break from the relationship to figure out who I am. The poem considers the possibility of stepping outside of the pain and reconnecting with my mother.

5. "Labyrinth" is a metaphor of being lost and trying to find a way through. This poem is an image of dealing with loss and sadness when not talking to my mom.

6. "Genie in a Bottle" is the spiritual awakening of realizing that my thoughts of my ex-fiancé and the fantasy of getting married to him no longer consumed me. After the breakup, I threw the necklace and his check into the Coralville Dam in Iowa. A fisherman found the bottle and then shipped it back to him a day before Valentine's Day. I promise that this is a true story.

7. The "Goodbyes" poem talks about grief. "Grandma's Birthday" is dedicated to my grandmother who passed away on July 4, 2009.

8. The next set of poems— "Who Am I?," "Tired of Losing," "Love from a Parent's Point of View," "The Sponsor," and "Let Go"—is about the hard work of recovery, experiencing pain, exploring connections to others, and particularly rediscovering myself and my connection to God.

9. "Goodbye Scale" and "Off the Wagon" introduce the work of recovering from an eating disorder and talk about the process of dealing with disordered eating.

10. "Maggie" is about a new connection with my cat and how when I have felt the urge to disappear, she has comforted me.

11. "Cry for Help" and "Relapse" are about my struggle with my eating disorder and asking God for help. I have learned in recovery to call for support even when I feel embarrassed or ashamed.

12. "Sensei" means "mentor." This poem is about losing money while starting a business to mentor kids. I felt a lot of hurt and anger at the time.

13. The next two poems, "Friendship" and "Carma," are reflecting on my current friendship and situation with my car. The situation with my car is the metaphor of my life where I try to escape feelings with destructive behaviors. I have learned I need to sit with my feelings and like myself in every situation.

14. "You Don't Know Me, Boss" is part of a new phase of starting to reflect on the larger outer world again: relationships. I struggled with my self-doubts and overcame them.

Introduction

15. "Missing You" is about my friend who went into relapse while I was staying sober, about my sitting with feelings and hoping we would meet again. This was very painful.

16. "Dayenu" is a poem of gratitude. A pastor taught me the phrase and it really resonated with me.

17. "A Thousand Pounds" allowed me to see my eating disorder in a positive light. I shared my story and some poems at a meeting, and a man told me that I encouraged him to write.

18. "Note to Daggie" is a note my mom wrote to me after we reconnected. She wrote the note on a napkin, and I kept it.

19. "Lost Child" is just as it sounds. I was raised to be perfect, rarely get into trouble, and stay quiet. I avoided confrontation at any cost. I denied my feelings, so everyone around me thought I had my life together. I learned to block feelings at an early age.

20. "New Chapter, New Sponsor" is about losing a dear sponsor and getting another wonderful sponsor. Through lots of therapy and recovery, I was able to move on and get a new job.

21. "Before I Turn 40" and "I Am Available" are reflecting on my life in knowing myself better. I am available for myself and others.

22. "Hurricane Harvey" is a poem about coping with fear from the storm. I bought my first house right before the storm.

23. "My Meds" was written at the time when I had a hard time accepting that I had depression and needed medication. I cried in meetings, believing there was something wrong with me. I learned later that many other people in recovery were on medication too. I am not alone.

24. "Freedom" and "Eyes Wide Shut" showed that I couldn't see clearly and my therapist needed to guide me.

25. "I Commit to You (God)" and "Loving Letter to Me" are about my formal commitment to God as well as a loving letter to self, showing the remarkable triumph of spirit over pain.

26. "Georgia from Childhood" is about my best and only girlfriend in second grade. She had leukemia, and I bullied her. It took me years to get over how I treated her. Georgia taught me unconditional love, and I am forever grateful.

27. "A Wall, No Intimacy" is about my mirror of self. I listened to a girl in group therapy talk on the surface and realized that was what I sounded like when I had my walls up and couldn't be vulnerable.

28. "Sitting in Fear" is about knowing I need to leave my current job because the culture does not align with my values and my boss is quite narcissistic. I learned in recovery that I have choices and I don't have to like the situation, but I have to like myself in the situation. For this reason, I am not afraid to leave.

29. "Where Are You, God?," "Trust the Recovery Process," "Growing Up," "Connecting with Others," and "Future Story" are the final show of my present and future. The images of God are how I view God today.

Feelings
February 12, 2015

I hear a wedding
I cry "it used to be"
I feel a sting
Why was it me?

I used to think
Never letting go meant strong
Now I rethink
That I was so wrong

I tell a story
My shame, my pain, my fear
No pride, no glory
Just a stranger in the mirror

I want to know her
What makes her smile
Today she's in a blur
She has to wait a while

Answers will flow
Trust in God
Be new, learn, and grow
Let yourself feel odd

This Too Shall Pass

Let the tears run
Run, run themselves dry
It's okay to miss the sun
You don't have to try

Try to stop tears from flowing
Try, try to be tough
Try to keep going
When you don't feel good enough

Don't pretend anymore
Face the truth
Don't close the door
Don't need proof

Speak from the heart
All around is love
If you fall apart
You are guided from above

You don't have to feel alone
Reach out, keep going
You see now you have grown
You will keep growing and going and going

Journey
February 21, 2015

Life is a journey
Where am I going?
Will I feel worthy?
Will I continue growing?

I feel your love
When I am in the room
I start to speak of
All I think of is gloom

I miss him right now
I need to sleep
No wedding vows
It is okay to grieve

You will be okay
Try to enjoy the path
Share yourself, share your way
Don't calculate, no math

You have to let go
This is your way
To say goodbye to throw
A future away in May

This Too Shall Pass

He didn't fight for you
You deserve a fight
All he did was argue
He battled out of spite

It's okay to feel
Sit with your feelings, sit with your friend
Be patient to heal
You will be whole. You will mend.

Create Your Story
February 25, 2015

I miss you less than yesterday
I miss you more today
Will I ever get over you?
Will I ever stop missing you?

Bittersweet memories
That's what I am taking with me
When you listened to me
For a short while

I had to say goodbye
Goodbye just makes me cry
But we both know that
Goodbye is what we need

I believed in us
Making it every step of the way
I was wrong
To believe in a dream

I can't wish for a better past
Or rush to start a future
I am sitting and sitting
Letting the tears fall like rain

This Too Shall Pass

I walk with you until night
The memories and reminders are there
All I ever saw was you and I forever
Now I must start a new journey

I begin a new story
A story that is full of happiness
My own happiness
A story that doesn't know

Where am I going?
Just close your eyes
The sun will shine again
You will be alright

On My Own
April 11, 2015

Some days I wish Thursdays never came
I wish my feelings could be numb
Fridays, Saturdays, and Sundays too
I don't know what to do

Some days I wish I never loved
I can't seem to stop thinking of
All the feelings for those I lost
All the paths that I have crossed

Some days I miss talking to mom
I tell voices in my head to calm
Everything hit me so hard
I need to let go of safeguard

I have to fall when I fall
Climb when I climb back on the wall
My mistakes are my own
I am not alone

God has my back
Sponsor can guide me on track
The path is only mine
Stop being stubborn, listen to divine

This Too Shall Pass

The answers are not up to me
My path is what God sees
I am a little scared
No control, feel dared

When will I love me?
God, when will I see?
That I have a reason to be alive
That I can survive

Survive on my own
No distractions, trust the unknown
God has my back
Sponsor can guide me on track

Go Away
April 12, 2015

Today is the day
I want to go away
I was happy then
Now I feel only pain

I have so many memories
Times that I miss
Moments that I want to forget
Feelings that I don't want to feel

It's hard to be alone
To not have a best friend
To see and hug every day
Letting them know how special they are

It's not easy trusting in God
Some days I want to give up
On everything because
My heart is broken

Broken into a million pieces
How will I mend
When all I feel is pain
Deep, deep pain

This Too Shall Pass

God, please guide me
I am so lost
All I think to do
Is go to a meeting right now

Mother's Day
May 10, 2015

I love you, Mom, with all my heart
The 1000 miles away from you
In silence, a distance far apart
This change is all so very new

I want you to know I don't hate
I am not doing this out of spite
I am doing this to let go of the weight
I have been carrying all day and night

I thought I was alright
Until the silence started
My feelings started to excite
No longer felt guarded

I cried for my cat Cheetoh
Missing his unconditional love
He had such a soul
I feel his presence above

I cried getting your presents
Knowing you were thinking of me
To me it represents
Your love wants me happy and free

This Too Shall Pass

May 2, my wedding day
Turned out to be a day I flew
Balloon floating away
Sharing the joy all the way through

May 4, my honeymoon
I learned west coast swing
I felt so in tune
Like it was meant to be my thing

Today I cry
Thinking of all the pain
Because I said goodbye
Right now, I need to regain

Courage, strength, hope
To love and nurture me
No noise or voices, just cope
Love me, the one I see

Let go of the hurt
Dad's words that belittle
Any scars, any dirt
That left you and me brittle

With time I will forgive
First, I need to learn
Learn to learn to live
So that I can return

Labyrinth
May 11, 2015

I did this without Mom
Started from the beginning
Without knowing where I am going
Didn't know what to expect

I put one foot in front of the other
Followed one piece at a time
Took the next right step
Until I hit a dead end

I couldn't remember what I tried
Or didn't try
I wanted to keep going
Going to find my way out

I lost myself in grief
I cried until my eyes hurt
I felt so confused
I was lost in pain

My tears fell like rain
I prayed for God to help me
To teach me, to hold me, to guide me
Until I find my way out

This Too Shall Pass

Out of beating myself up
Out of being afraid to try
Out of giving up
On being the person I already am

I will be free
After I trust myself
And love myself enough to
Do the next right thing

I don't know where I am going
All I know is God is holding me
And will help me
Find my way out

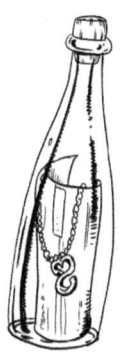

Genie in a Bottle
May 22, 2015

I had to let you go
The necklace wasn't mine
It belonged to your mistress
The check wasn't mine
It belonged to your mistress

They swam in a bottle
Through the Coralville Dam
Never to be found
Raging emotions, raging thoughts
I wanted to be strong

That day I freed myself
From bad karma
Unacceptable behavior, no trust
In the person I used to love
Who I freed myself of

A fisherman found the bottle
Shipped it to him
Before Valentine's Day
He is still a prisoner
I am a free woman

This Too Shall Pass

God is showing me the way
Teaching me to trust in myself
Love myself every day more
I am a capable woman
Trust and be open and learn

I am growing
Each day I am learning
To love myself more and more
I am growing
Grateful to be alive

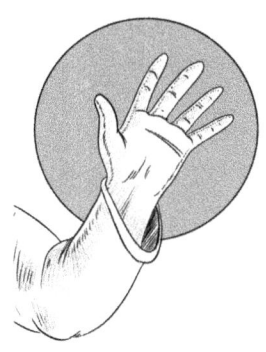

Goodbyes
June 24, 2015

Goodbye, little puppy Graham
Goodbye is what you need
Your life was cut short
Suffer no more

Goodbye old relationships
Goodbye is what I need
You are all that I've known
Start over, start fresh

Goodbye old habits
Goodbye is what I need
You stuck to me like glue
Stick no more

Goodbye character defects
Goodbye is what I need
You armored me with protection
Protect no more

Goodbye resentments
Goodbye is what I need
You kept me distant
Distance no more

This Too Shall Pass

Goodbye bullies
Goodbye is what I need
I took years of abuse
Abuse no more

Goodbye wishing for a better past
Goodbye is what I need
You kept me trapped
Stuck no more

Grandma's Birthday
July 4, 2015

The day before
I got a makeover
Laura took me to Sephora
I felt a positive aura

I wanted to feel good
Believe that I could
Ask for help
On how to put on makeup

I will celebrate with Laura
In a positive aura
Because I want to
Feel connected, do something new

Now I feel strong
I can go on
Feeling God's presence
Teaching me so many lessons

Today I feel beautiful
My life feels so suitable
Doing so much now
With a different view

This Too Shall Pass

Cooked Polish food
It felt so good
I did on my own
Being okay to be alone

Who Am I
July 27, 2015

Am I a cold bitch?
Some kind of witch?
I don't know anymore
I just want to close the door

I don't feel strong
This is a sad song
I want to give up
Ignore me, close up

All I want is to hide
I don't have any pride
Just down in the hole
Trying to find my soul

My dad is sick
I can hear time tick
I'm not ready to say goodbye
I would rather it be me to die

I feel so alone
Raw to bare bone
Afraid to talk to Mom
Afraid what it might stir

This Too Shall Pass

Is my sponsor good for me?
Am I too blind to see?
I need to be told
Even if it feels cold

God, I ask for clarity
I ask for purity
I'm down on my knees
Only you who sees

My sadness and pain
Tears running down like rain
My car insurance went up
I feel like I'm in the dump

I want to smile
Even if I wait awhile
I want to forgive me
The one I see

Every day I am with me
Who I see
Who I don't love
Only you love me from above

Stay with me
The one you see
Love me, nurture me
Just let me be

I miss my mom
I play that old song
Wishing Mom was here
To avoid who I see in the mirror

Who Am I

The letter to Mom
Felt shitty and not calm
It's to process my thoughts
To maybe connect the dots

I'm mad at sponsor
She is a monster
Thought she was great
Like we connected through fate

Doesn't she know what I thought?
My stomach is in a knot
I have started new
What else can I do?

Tired of Losing
August 23, 2015

No matter what I say or do
I feel like a loser
I don't feel worthy
I don't feel like I belong

I talk too much
I listen too little
I feel hurt when I hear "no"
I feel rejected

I don't know much about love
How to really love myself
I continue beating myself with a stick
The pain just keeps on growing

God, I am defeated
I am tired of losing
This battle with myself and against myself
Tired of being me

My thinking and feelings are historical
Thinking and doing things my way
Is getting me nowhere
Listening to you, God, sitting with pain all day

Tired of Losing

I am telling my truth
I surrender, I am powerless
My head wants to run away from feelings
Listening to you, God, letting tears fall like rain

I need to continue asking for help
Sponsor and supervisor show they care
Because they tell me what I need
Not what I want to hear

I will let them love me
Trust in their guidance
Until I can love me
Until I can trust myself

I want to start winning
With your help, God
I feel like I am winning
By riding the storm to heal

Awareness – I admitted I am powerless over feelings and thoughts
Acceptance – In my 10-second window, I let God in and didn't run away from feelings
Action – I sat with my feelings all day and cried
Feeling "unworthy" and "unlovable" are my default feelings that come up.

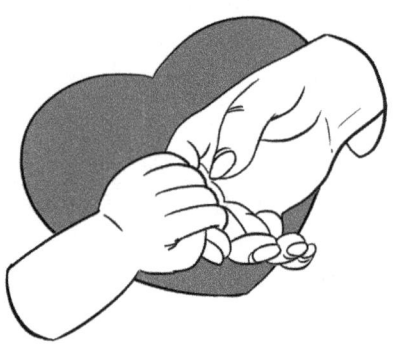

Love from a Parent's Point of View
September 2, 2015

I respect your wishes
To not call or contact you
Even if this causes me great pain
This is about your growth
Find out who you are
What makes you smile

I respect your wishes
To let you go through pain
Cry all the tears that come
I can't feel for you
I can't stop your tears
I can't make you happy

I respect your wishes
To let you work your program
Find the support you need
Work with sponsor
Work with therapist
Find your way to peace

I respect your wishes
To leave you alone
Even if I don't want to

Love from a Parent's Point of View

Because in the end
None of this is between you and me
It's between you and God

The Sponsor
September 21, 2015

I came in brokenhearted
With a soul so bare
What was I supposed to do?
Where was I supposed to go?

God spoke to me that day
Do not be afraid, Dagmar
Go on and ask her, ask her
Forget the shame and the pain

Do you know she is my sponsor?
There is no I in this journey
Walk alongside, we shall walk
Or I will be empty-handed

I am not alone in the darkness
On this long, long road ahead
There is love on my journey
I got no clue where I am going

God, I can't live without you
I don't know where I am going
I won't walk alone anymore
Please help me, walk with me

The Sponsor

Thank you for loving me
Thank you for showing me the way
Giving me the strength to ask her
Forget the shame and pain

She knows where I have been
Not going, back there again
It is all black
I say no to that

She is my sponsor, my mentor
I knock and she answers the door
I ask and she guides me
Seeking to find the answers

She knows where I have been
Not going back there again
It is all black
I say no to that

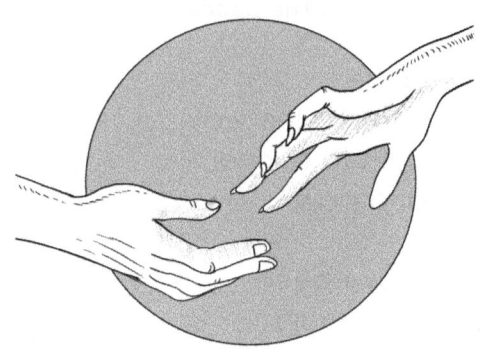

Let Go
October 4, 2015

I didn't know love
Until I let my girlfriend go
The tears fell like rain
Couldn't stop them in the meeting

It hurt so bad
To hear her say "I love you"
Then turn her back on me
Because she didn't get her way

I don't want to kiss her ass
I want to stay true to my principles
Even if hurts so bad
From someone who I thought loved me

I love my girlfriend
I'll let her find her way
While I am true to me
Respect myself in a way I never have before

Frustration showed up again
Learned that I live to work
I don't want to live to work
I don't want to be a workaholic

Let Go

I don't want one in my life
I know one thing, I want balance

Why, God, did three people show up?
All with a past that reminded me
Of my past
Neil and Dad with workaholic behavior
Rodrigo addicted to women
Harry an addict like Stephen and Michael
Reminded me of my past

I spoke up
Got them figured out right away
Please, God, help me
Bring healthy people into my life
Help me find interests
In a healthy way
I need your help

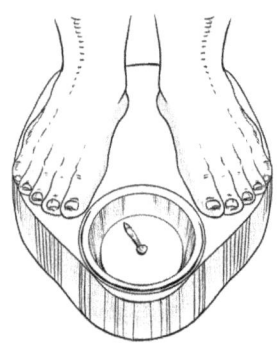

Goodbye, Scale
October 5, 2015

You served me for so long
Told me I am everything
Told me I am nothing
Confused the shit out of me

I felt I could prove myself
Show you and the world
I am an expert in food and exercise
I know something

People came to me
Asked me questions about health
I never felt so sure
Or proud in my life than on this topic

Now I don't feel so sure
That I am healthy
Never told people the truth
About what it really took to be me

I ran away to hide pain
Burned everything I ate and more
To prove to my scale
I can succeed in everything

Goodbye, Scale

Now with me changing
What will I be good at?
How can I help people?
When this is all I have known

I feel like a liar
I lied to myself
And to everyone
That I am so good in this

My disorder got the best of me
It has taken over my life
All I think about is food and exercise
I need to say goodbye

God, please help me
Please love me
Until I can love myself
Please help me find me

Please help me be okay
Let go of numbers on clothes
I hate numbers now
Numbers make me sick

Please help me find meetings
Find the support I need
To be okay with me
To find peace, happiness, and closure

Off the Wagon
October 29, 2015

I am so tired
It's been a long road
All windy and shit
No clue where I am going

I know where I've been
I could go there again
Here I go again
Going back to where I've been

I say no to that
Don't want to go back
It's all black
I say no to that

I hear of this thing called trust
Don't hide in the ditch
Trust my support
Trust in God

God knows everything
Tell God it all
Talk it through in recovery
Don't hide in the ditch

Off the Wagon

I know where I've been
I could go there again
Here I go again
Going back to where I've been

I say no to that
Don't want to go back
It's all black
I say no to that

Abstinence is a bitch
The idea feels great
Doing is exhausting
Sometimes want to quit

I know where I've been
I could go there again
Here I go again
Going back to where I've been

I say no to that
Don't want to go back
It's all black
I say no to that

Maggie
November 13, 2015

The evenings are very scary
All I feel is sadness
I cry myself to sleep
Nothing gives me joy

I don't know why I'm here
Why, God, is this happening?
Did you lose me, God?
Do you even know I exist?

I thought about flying
Dropping off my balcony
I wouldn't feel anything
The pain would disappear

Then I look at my cat Maggie
Who is so shy and innocent
Who needs me like I need her
She reminds me that I'm not alone

My support and big bro remind me too
They love me
Even when I'm a mess
They give me strength to go on

Maggie

Monday blues until Friday
I can't snap out of this
Unless I start using my drug
Which I crave for less and less

What used to work is gone
All that's left is pain
Great deal of pain and sadness
That I am powerless over

To ask for more help
To ask for a psychiatrist
Feels so scary and weak
I don't know what else to do

I am no longer going to fight
Against getting more help
I hope you are with me, God
Because I feel very alone

Then I look at my cat Maggie
Who is shy and innocent
Who needs me like I need her
She reminds me I am not alone

Cry for Help
November 19, 2015

I cried every night
Hated the morning sun
I didn't want to wake up
I didn't want to live

I started going to meetings
I listened to the shares
Even if I didn't want to fit in
I was accepted with open arms

All I wanted was to belong
To not feel so much shame
For gaining so much weight
To stop feeling ugly

Sponsor told me to talk in meetings
I need to get phone numbers
Start calling people
Let people get to know me

I started to call people
This week I called my people
No one judged me
No one laughed at me

Cry for Help

I started to share in meetings
I cried for help
Lindsay is going grocery shopping with me
Support is going to lunch with me

People listen to me
They share their deepest shame
New people in my life
I feel so much love

There are people who love me
My supervisor doesn't know me
And maybe wants what's best for me
Showing in the only way she knows how

Giving her what she wants
Stop battling and trying to win
Be honest and keep reaching out
To new friends, new family

God loves you
Brought these people into your life
Show them your heart
Show them your courage

Ask for help
Don't be afraid
You don't have to hide the pain
The answers will come

Relapse
December 6, 2015

I am in control
I have a good plan
Soothing my soul
Because I can

I did this alone
No logic at all
I didn't want to be known
I didn't reach out and call

My obsession took place
I needed the fix
Everything was a haze
I needed it quick

I indulged and it felt good
Then it felt bad
I wasn't in a good mood
Soon I felt so very sad

The miles I walked
In such a daze
A prisoner, feeling locked
Thursday is a haze

Relapse

I would have stolen that day
I was so hungry
All I wanted was my way
It was all about me

Now I can't say that
My last relapse was March 26
I can say that
I don't care for that fix

I thank God for teaching me
That I need help
Keeps me honest, let's me see
There is another way

Sensei
December 6, 2015

Everyone tells me
You have some plan for me
How can I believe you?
When all I feel is sad

My soul has died
Hundred times over again
With all the goodbyes
The sun ain't coming out

No no the sun ain't shining
What am I supposed to do?
Where am I going?
Why am I here?

You keep showing me something
All week, sensei
Unless I am going mad
All I think about is sensei

How do I get started?
Again, after fucking up so bad
I could have done this before
But I fucked up bad

Sensei

I went down sinking my ship
Sometimes wanted to die
Didn't believe in myself then
Still don't believe in myself now

I can't do this alone
I hope you know what you are doing
I have lost my tread
Please help me

My soul has died
Hundred times over again
With all the goodbyes
The sun ain't coming out

Friendship
December 18, 2015

I am on your mind
You are on mine too
I hope you are okay
Can't wait to see you next

Spending time on my own
Learning to be with me
When I see you next
You aren't there to fill my void

You are there for support
Whatever I decide
Even if it's crazier than shit
You don't judge me

I have to hit my rock bottoms
Which got me into recovery
Yet that doesn't matter to you
You ask when can I see you next?

Spending time on my own
Learning to be with me
When I see you next
You aren't there to fill my void

Friendship

I can be myself
Tell you the truth of why I can't see you
You ask me if I feel better
I feel whole

No more lying, cheating, or deceiving
I can be a mess
Cry and be who I am
You are here for me

Spending time on my own
Learning to be with me
When I see you next
You aren't there to fill my void

Carma
January 3, 2016

I met you at the dealership
Your body was too shiny
I came that day to see
If you and I were meant to be

That day I kept my secrets from you
Never told you the truth
And in the explosions, you saw
How I was so vulnerable and raw

Yet I can't stop
I don't care about you anymore
I am mad at you for
Seeing my inner core

You remind me of the past
I don't want to go there anymore
I am reminded of what used to be
Those ideas no longer suit me

How do I accept you?
When I am the one to blame
I chose you instead of the other
Wishing you weren't attached to my mother

Carma

You don't deserve the abuse
The horrible things you went through
Is true because I don't accept you
I don't even like you

You remind me of Iowa
All I see is my mom
My first boyfriend helped me
Programmed your settings can't you see

What you are doing to me?
How can I be free?
When I don't want to be
Stuck with you and me

As long as I have gas
And you are still running strong
We have to learn how to be
With each other you and me

You aren't doing anything to me
I need to set myself free
Need to learn how to be
Loving to you and me

The only way I see
Is to pretend I love me so
I can be gentle and kind to me
Letting the resentment and anger go free

You Don't Know Me, Boss
January 7, 2016

You don't know
What is good for me so
Why do you drive?
When I feel so alive

I finally get to see
That side of me
That you try to kill
When I just climbed the hill

To finally get here
To finally get here
I just nod my head
At whatever you said

Thank you. I repeat your thought
So I don't get caught
Arguing with you
Because that's what I do

I will take what you teach
To help me reach
My very best
I'm on a quest

You Don't Know Me, Boss

You don't know
What's good for me so
Why do you drive?
When I feel so alive

Why do I explain to you?
What I'm about to do
Why do I feel so insecure?
You don't even hear

The tickle in my voice
Because I am making a choice
To make learning fun
Like it's never been done

You don't know
What's good for me so
Why do you drive?
When I feel so alive

You want the same
Which is very lame
I love creating new
That's what I will continue to do

You do teach me how to plan
Even though I can't stand
You finally feel good
Saying that I should

Follow your lead
To plant a seed
Into something I fight
Now I see the light

This Too Shall Pass

Even if you don't know
What's good for me
You can continue to drive
I will still feel alive

Because I feel my way out
Out of this hideout
It's called creating new
That's what I do

No one can stop me
Can't you see
This is me
I feel so happy and free

Missing You
March 30, 2016

I've been so many places in my life
I've played so many games and lost
I've made so many mistakes
Digging a grave for myself
But we're parted now and I'm singing this song for you

I don't love you any less for leaving
I've always felt so sad and good with you
I hope you can see
But we're parted now and I am singing this song for you

You taught me the truth withholding nothing
You reached out when I wanted to hide
You showed me strength, determination
You wanted peace so bad
But we're parted now and I am singing this song for you

Listen to this song cause my love is hiding
I love you in a place where there is no distance
I love you for you will always be my friend
Remember when we were together
Cause we're parted now and I am singing this song
   for you

This Too Shall Pass

You taught me the truth withholding nothing
You reached out when I wanted to hide
You showed me strength, determination
You wanted peace so bad
But we're parted now and I am singing this song for you

Listen to this song 'cause my love is hiding
I love you in a place where there is no distance
I love you for you will always be my friend
Remember when we were together
Cause we're parted now and I am singing this song for you

I hope to see you again
I hope to see you again

'Cause we're parted now and I am singing this song for you

Dayenu
June 19, 2016

If you have given me a sponsor who listens just for today and tomorrow walks away, Dayenu

If you had given me a rewarding job with no increase in pay and I remain a consultant, Dayenu

If you had given me a tennis coach and not taken my chance away to play, Dayenu

If you had given me a cat who is my best friend and no children of my own, Dayenu

If you had given me a chance to do a living amend through starting my business and not supplied wealth, Dayenu

If you had given me a community who loves me as I am and not a man, Dayenu

If you had given me a mother and father and not different parents, Dayenu

If you had relieved me of my eating disorder and not taken it away forever, Dayenu

If you had given me a car that is reliable and affordable and not something else, Dayenu

If you had given me an apartment in Montrose and not near Memorial Park, Dayenu

If you had relieved my depression and anxiety for today and not taken it away forever, Dayenu

It would have been enough. You are enough. I am enough.

A Thousand Pounds
November 25, 2016

I carried a thousand pounds
Of pain and sorrow and grief
I know where I've been
Not sure where I am going

I look into the mirror
A stranger stood there
Who can this be?
It is the new me

Can I tell myself?
You've come a long way
It's okay to feel this way
It's okay to be sad

One day you'll wake up
See the people you helped
See the love you've gotten
For doing nothing

Yet it's a big deal
I did something
I stayed on a course
Didn't give up

A Thousand Pounds

Today I carry a thousand pounds
Of joy, love, and thank you
To all that helped me
To God who can see

The strength in me
The persistence in me
The courage in me
The love in me

I helped one man
Start writing again
How can that be?
How can that be?

Note to Daggie – Reunion with Mom
November 28, 2016

I have discovered
The true meaning
(Finally ☺) to
Thanksgiving while
Spending time with
You in Houston.
You've been open and
present and that is
how I understand
LOVE. I am grateful
beyond these words. Mom

Lost Child
December 15, 2016

Sorry my name is Dagmar
Sorry for taking up your time
Sorry our paths crossed
Sorry you even saw me

I'd rather be in the shadow
Where I am safe
Never to be hurt
Never to be heard

If you really knew me
You'd say I am a liar
A bitch too
So why do you care?

To talk to me
When you know I feel scared?
Of being myself
It's easier to pretend

I'd rather be in the shadow
Where I am safe
Never to be hurt
Never to be heard

New Chapter, New Sponsor
March 21, 2017

I was proud to say
You were my sponsor
The one I could call
When I felt beat down

I cried when you told me
"I'm no longer going to sponsor you"
What did I do or say?
How can I change your mind?

God helped me talk to you
I guess you gave me all you can
Now I need someone different
Someone to work steps with

I have someone new
It's not who I chose
Less available than you
Showing me a different way

I still feel shock
I cried after my interview
You are no longer my sponsor
I got the new job

Before I Turn 40
August 24, 2017

1. I want to earn at least $110,000 per year. I deserve this based on my school and experience according to research.
2. I want to be an employee, not a contractor, and a lead or manager in Learning and Development.
3. I want to own a house.
4. I want to max out my retirement, if not get close to maxing it out.
5. I want to be a sponsor.
6. I want to start dating.
7. I want to explore at least one new hobby and interest.
8. I want to finish reading the books on my dresser.
9. I want to travel and explore new places.

I Am Available
August 27, 2017

Please hold me, love me
Tell me everything will be okay
Please don't leave me
When I feel so sad

I know I ain't perfect
My boss said loud and clear
That I've got to change my ways
I've got a lot to learn

I felt it coming
Something didn't feel right
I wanted my therapist and friends
To see me, hear me, tell me

Please hold me, love me
Tell me everything will be okay
Please don't leave me
When I feel so sad

I'm down on my knees
Tears rolling down my face
Nothing makes sense
I'm asking to show me the way

I Am Available

I've stripped the part of me
That looks real tough
Wants everyone to see
I got it together

Who am I, God?
When I don't feel so tough
When all I can do is listen
And tell the truth

Please hold me, love me
Tell me everything will be okay
Please don't leave me
When I feel so sad

Hurricane Harvey
August 27, 2017

I'm sitting in my new office
Cabinets and desk smell of oak trees
I pretend I'm in the woods
Feeling safe and so much peace

The truth is I have no power
Rain is pouring like no tomorrow
I feel scared
Not knowing when power will turn on

This is my first house
I ain't got a clue what to do
So, I sit and write
Pretending I'm someplace else

I got the candles lit bright
I got the bonfire going
Enjoying the company of others
Everyone talking about God

I feel so safe
Enjoying the sound of rain
I've got cabin fever
God is keeping me safe

Hurricane Harvey

Electricity just went on
I'm so happy right now
Thank you, God
For listening like you always do

Please keep my friends safe
Some got it really bad
May get flooded or worse
God is keeping my friends safe

My Meds
October 16, 2017

I am told you are good for me
I don't want to swallow you
Cause I got this under control
I can handle my feelings and thoughts

I want to forget about you
I ain't got time
Cause there's nothing, there's nothing you
Can do for me
That I can't do for myself

I don't need you
I don't care about you
I hate you so much
You remind me I am fucked up

I am told you are good for me
I don't want to swallow you
Cause I got this under control
I can handle my feelings and thoughts

I want to find another relationship
Move on because I don't need you
You remind me I am fucked up
Let me have some pride

Freedom
October 17, 2017

Hey, therapist, I feel so guilty
For comparing myself to you
I know you're feeling sad
About my week spent in so much pain

The stories I made up
Took away from my freedom
Took away all my choices
All I could hear were the voices

There were times I wanted to ignore them
There were times I nearly won
But then they came back stronger
I had nowhere to run

Please forgive me for my thoughts
I hope you understand and see
That you were a beautiful person
That led me to my freedom

If I had anything to give you
It would be to show you
What you mean to me
By accepting the one you see

This Too Shall Pass

I have a life that is a miracle
You have helped me get this far
Now I talk to Mom and Dad and bro
When it used to be so hard

I have a new home
New friends from recovery and church
Now I can do a soul search
And see who is that hiding girl

I hope you forgive me
It took courage for me to say
What was on my mind today
Now I just want to say

I love you
Thanks for being you
I hope you can forgive me
For this session that you helped me through

Eyes Wide Shut
October 18, 2017

My eyes can finally see
What the hell's wrong with me
My mouth can say what's on my mind
Not knowing what my therapist will find

My mouth told her I am insecure
All I was feeling was so much fear
What would she say or do
If she knew that I knew

The secret of waiving her fee
Giving special people sessions for free
Why does she care about me?
I don't exist, don't you see

Money is a way to show love
This is what I know of true love
She told me my relationships will break
All will end up in a heartbreak

I thought she didn't love me
Cause I didn't get help for free
I learned that's for people in need
Not for people like me with greed

This Too Shall Pass

Why do you see something in me?
That I don't even care to see
Even when I am hard to love
You will find something to be proud of

I exhaust all my friends
Then I end up doing amends
I blast text messages to my therapist
Everything is a blur mist

I am like a drunk on fire
Nothing at all to admire
I am crazy and shit
I hit send and transmit

She gets the fire
Nothing at all to admire
I want to stop this cycle
For once I want it to be final

I now see my old ways
I give my therapist huge praise
For not leaving me in pain
I now can take away her blame

I Commit to You (God)
October 19, 2017

Baptized at Mercy Street Methodist Church, October 21, 2017

It's not over between you and me
I choose you over and over
Even when I say, "I am quitting you"
Even when I ask, "Where are you, God?"

I don't got a punch line
Or anything profound to say
I just know there is some magic
In the relationship between you and me

You led me to a wonderful therapist
I told you when I stopped my meds
You remind me to go to meetings
You introduce me to new friends

Mercy Street got broken folks like me
They don't got a punch line
Or anything profound to say
Their soul is so loving

I didn't think I belonged here
My head was down hoping you don't see

This Too Shall Pass

My heart was broken a million times over
You showed me that I do belong

I don't got a punch line
Or anything profound to say
I just know there is some magic
In the relationship between you and me

Today I have amazing friends
Support that keeps me real
God of my understanding
A house that I can call home

Today I can see my wonderful parents
I love my brothers too
And my cat Maggie who saved my life
I feel so grateful for my life today

It's not over between you and me
I commit to you over and over
Even when I say, "I am quitting you"
Even when I ask, "Where are you, God"?

Dating Again – When I Date Again
October 23, 2017

1. Don't try to change me.
2. Don't tell me how to feel or think. Don't put me down.
3. Don't keep your exes around.
4. DO keep your word.
5. DO have boundaries.
6. DO be direct and honest.
7. DO have a foundation with God.
8. DO support yourself. I value people who know how to save and spend wisely.
9. DO respect me.
10. DO listen and show that you like me in ways other than giving gifts or money.

Loving Letter to Me
October 23, 2017

Dear Dagmar,

You are one of the most determined and brave people that I know. I've watched you grow over the last five years since you entered recovery. You were a scared young woman who left her fiancé not knowing what would happen next. You were willing to get a sponsor and start working the steps. You started your journey in finding "you" even though you didn't love yourself yet. You let others love you, and you trusted them because you didn't trust your strength. I knew you were strong, lovable, and a joy to be around. You, in time, would know that too. You are direct, honest, and dependable. You are funny too. Your writing is a gift. You can feel others' pain when you tap into it. You are sensitive even if at times you try to be strong and cover up the pain with jokes or being a rebellious teenager. You need love like everyone else, and deep inside you know you are the only one who can give yourself love and a pat on the back. Don't ever doubt your gifts. If you come back to this letter, realize you have come so far. You fought against therapy, meds, church, group therapy, programs, and getting sponsors. Your willingness and openness allowed you to experience God through these channels. Don't ever stop questioning what's right for you. Only God knows what's right. Keep up the great work. Keep practicing your tools and keep your chin up. You are beautiful inside and out. Grandma and Pete would be proud of you. The man of your dreams will find you. Wait and keep smiling.

Love,

Inner Wisdom

Georgia from Childhood
October 24, 2017

Oh, Georgia, you're on my mind
If you are still here
Do you even remember me?
Do you have any loving memories?

I remember you
You were a happy girl
Never really showed me
What you were really going through

You showed me how to eat Oreos
Breaking the cookie into two
Then dipping into whole milk
Eating more than just a few

You showed me your favorite meal
You love noodles in butter
I love how happy they made you feel
Enjoying every single string

I'm sorry for my words
I wish I could take them back
You were my best friend
That I didn't even deserve

This Too Shall Pass

There is a Santa Claus
That will listen to your every wish
Praying your heart will be filled with joy
That you definitely deserve

Oh, Georgia, you're on my mind
If you are still here
Do you even remember me?
Do you have any loving memories?

If you didn't make it
I know you won't suffer anymore
All the times you weren't in school
I missed you so much

I had too much pride
To admit you were my best friend
Thought you were a loser
You were my best friend

A Wall, No Intimacy
November 8, 2018

I don't know you
When you speak you
Don't say a word
Just talk gibberish

I can't see you
For who you are
With turtles and dogs
And vivid stories

What is the point
To talk to talk
I can't hear you
No word is said

I don't know you
When you speak you
Don't say a word
Just talk gibberish

What is the point
When I show up
I speak my truth
All that I have

This Too Shall Pass

When you speak you
Don't show real you
Why are you here?
Why am I here?

Why are you seen?
Why are you affirmed?
Why does your time
Matter more than my time?

I feel so ignored
I feel so bored
This is my trigger
To act out again

I don't know you
When you speak you
Don't say a word
Just talk gibberish

I don't like you
'Cause you aren't real
I don't feel safe
In this room now

Things have to change
I have to change
Group or something
'Cause it isn't working

I don't know you
When you speak you
Don't say a word
Just talk gibberish

Sitting in Fear
November 11, 2018

I don't know I don't know
Why am I really here?
When all I feel is fear
Of changing my old ways

Water is supposed to bring peace
Calming my ass down
Sip it down
Now I can think clear

My life ain't alright
I'm back to a blur
Can't see my true mirror
Or who I want to become

I don't know I don't know
Why am I really here?
When all I feel is fear
Of changing my old ways

I guess I will find out
For now with God's help
I will serve others
While balancing my needs

This Too Shall Pass

No I will sit
Sit in my fear
Do nothing just write
Write, just write

What can I do different?
Speak up in the moment
Ask can you show me?
This will set me free

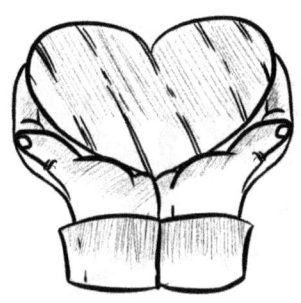

Where Are You, God?
November 12, 2018

All my life I struggled trusting and understanding this mystical thing called God. When I got into recovery I resented people talking about God or their Higher Power. I felt so much anger and pain that people spoke so well about God and I was miserable. Now I understand God in my own way. When I am closest to God I see an angel, a butterfly, and an elephant.

Trust the Recovery Process
November 15, 2018

The angel is what I have tattooed on my right hip. She helps guide me and keeps me safe from dangerous situations. The angel has experienced the dark and light with me as you can see by rough and smooth wings. The adjectives describe what the angel gives to me.

Growing Up
November 18, 2018

When I get a desire or sobriety chip, I always think of trying to change my ways and grow. The butterfly reminds me to keep developing, changing my old ways, and being direct with my intentions.

Serenity Prayer: "God, grant me the serenity to accept the things I cannot change, courage to change the things I can, and the wisdom to know the difference."

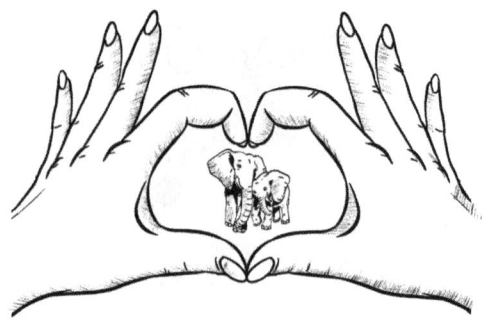

Connecting with Others
November 30, 2018

To be vulnerable and ask others for help used to terrify me. I didn't want others to know me and to think of me as weak. Now I have the closest friends because of my willingness to be honest and open with others.

I love studying elephants because they are so caring and social toward each other. They remind me to be vulnerable, process feelings and thoughts with others, and to ask for help.

Future Story
December 21, 2018

    I can't believe that I have the life I have always wanted. I am married to an imperfect man who is faithful, honest, goes to church with me, works on himself, and truly loves me. We live in my house I bought in Montrose with my cat Maggie. He is intellectually curious and stimulates me with his brain. I spend my alone time doing art and writing poems. Singing and piano have continued to interest me, and I've mastered a few performances. My job as a Learning Professional keeps me busy, though I make time for recovery. I still play tennis with Coach Dan. I've been able to heal nicely from the foot surgery and took up hiking again. My mom and I went to Yosemite and the Pacific Trail. My husband loves hiking, peaceful nature, and history, so we went to Poland and Italy recently. I finally made it to Auschwitz and it made me feel grateful that I am alive and so are the people around me. I also went to the major tennis opens. I love my girlfriends. Grateful for my life today.

Resources for Addiction Issues

Adult Children of Alcoholics offers a program of recovery for those who grew up in dysfunctional homes and is a safe space to grieve childhood and heal from the trauma. To find a meeting near you, visit https://adultchildren.org.

Al-Anon offers support and fellowship for friends and families of alcoholics. To find a meeting near you, visit al-anon.org.

Alcoholics Anonymous is a fellowship of men and women who share their experience, strength, and hope with one another that they may solve their common problems and help others recover from alcoholism. To find a meeting near you, visit aa.org.

Anorexia Bulimia Anonymous offers a program of recovery from anorexia and bulimia using the Twelve Steps and Twelve Traditions of OA (Overeaters Anonymous). Worldwide meetings and other tools provide a fellowship of experience, strength, and hope where members respect one another's anonymity. OA charges no dues or fees; it is self-supporting through member contributions. To find a meeting near you, visit aba12steps.org.

Codependents Anonymous offers support and fellowship for men and women whose common purpose is to develop healthy relationships. Living the program allows you to become increasingly honest with yourself about personal histories and codependent behaviors. To find a meeting near you, visit coda.org.

Overeaters Anonymous offers a program of recovery from compulsive overeating using the Twelve Steps and Twelve Traditions of OA. Worldwide meetings and other tools provide a fellowship of experience, strength, and hope where members respect one another's anonymity. OA charges no dues or fees; it is self-supporting through member contributions. To find a meeting near you, visit oa.org.

Sex Addiction Anonymous offers a program of recovery to stop addictive sexual behavior and to help others recover from sexual addiction. To find a meeting near you, visit saa-recovery.org.

Sex and Love Addicts Anonymous
Sex and Love Addicts Anonymous, or S.L.A.A., is a program for anyone who suffers from an addictive compulsion to engage in or avoid sex, love, or emotional attachment. The program uses the Twelve Steps and Twelve Traditions adapted from Alcoholics Anonymous to recover from these compulsions. To find a meeting near you, visit slaafws.org.

A Note about the Author

Dagmar Eva Kusiak's recovery remains the primary focus and inspiration for her book. She has struggled with a learning disability, experienced many failed relationships, faced eating disorders, fantasized about death, studied education and psychology, lost and discovered God, and experienced the pain and pleasure of love. She is a Learning and Development Professional and runs support meetings at recovery centers for women. She joined the rooms of recovery in December 2012, and it wasn't until February 2014, that she started searching for her purpose by writing poems. She lives in Houston in the "creative mecca" called Montrose. This is her first book.

www.ingramcontent.com/pod-product-compliance
Lightning Source LLC
Chambersburg PA
CBHW070207100426
42743CB00013B/3080